Ache
is a
Passport

Ache
is a
Passport

*love letters to survivors
of spiritual abuse*

Amanda Dzimianski

for all the little ones
who spent childhood
terrified of hell

then grew up
and realized
they already
lived there

Table of Contents

a note from the author

Hey, friend.

Spiritual abuse—light stuff, huh?

Often when people hear the term "spiritual abuse," they think of molestation and sexual abuse by members of clergy or religious leadership[1](with excellent reason). However, while spiritual abuse may absolutely be used to groom someone for sexual abuse, spiritual abuse itself is a broader category.

It's a term that isn't always clear-cut. But here is an explanation of exactly what I mean when I use the phrase spiritual abuse:

the manipulation, suppression, silencing, restriction, domination, and/or active

----

1 A video from Dr. Laura Anderson, PhD, LMFT, helped me recognize the need to differentiate between sexual and spiritual abuse, and was the catalyst for the definition of spiritual abuse in this section. Dr. Laura Anderson [@drlauraeanderson]. "When I tell people that I work with folks who have religious trauma..." *Instagram*, 23, Sept. 2022, https://www.instagram.com/reel/Ci20dDDpxi4/.

oppression of individuals, their voices,
beliefs, and free will
by weaponizing
internal and external shame,
ostracization, groupthink, and fear
(particularly of an unseen, spiritual realm),
for the purpose of
enabling a religious sect/institution/
system/individual to maintain a subjective
moral or doctrinal 'purity', protecting
clerical reputation & livelihood, building
organizational wealth, and/or
retaining/gaining societal power & control.

That is how I understand the concept.

The poems in this collection are written for people who grew up in religious contexts that checked some, if not all, of the boxes represented in the definition above.

For you who have spent some or all of your life

-bargaining with a deity
-people-pleasing in the name of faith
-tamping down your every desire
-judging your own emotions

-fearing the fires of hell or the imminence
of an apocalypse
-rebranding—or ignoring—your intuition
-suffering to keep others comfortable

-hiding your truest self underneath layers
of acceptability as defined by your
community
-pursuing your religion's brand of holiness
at the expense of your own curiosity,
dreams, ambitions, and/or physical and
mental health

…these poems are for you.

One more thing. The poems in this book
contain language and concepts found
within the western evangelical Christian
framework (though they may also apply in
other religious contexts).

Since you picked up this book, I'm
assuming you carry some scars from
squeezing your soul into that box, or a
similar one, and some words and ideas
may already leave a bitter taste in your
mouth.

I'd never want you to be blindsided by those terms and phrases that have already caused harm. Words hold power, and that's why they can be weapons.

So, if you choose to read, when you encounter any of the words used against you in the past, know that I mean the opposite of what your body integrated during Sunday sermons.

For myself, I'm choosing to use religious expression in some of these poems in order to reclaim it. No single system of belief deserves to carry a monopoly on the astronomical themes of life, death, truth, beauty, righteousness, etc.

We were handed definitions without consent, and our curiosity was razed. I choose to twist the meanings back on themselves, and give the words a chance to shapeshift into better things.

May you feel seen, heard, and held. You are worthy of love.

content warning

religious verbiage & symbolism
spiritual abuse & manipulation
coarse language

eucharist

crushed soul of grapes
and chalk-paper bread
pass
past you

somehow
silver plates
and plastic cups,
supposed symbols
of what it means
to give it all away,
become a holy
hoarding-fest

one day
you wake up
and walk out

because
the table
has lost its luster
and you
have found your appetite

more

you were born for this, dear heart

this wrestling
waiting
wondering

you were born for this because
you were made for more, more
than what you have known
so far

more
is your birthright
more
will be your legacy

more is the meaning
stitched
on the back sides of your
ever-stretching
moments

more is right here, right now,
through the thread loops
of the forever-expanding
canvas of your mind

more is not where you're from
but I promise,
it's where you're going

count the cost

when you slice
through
the tethers
sever yourself
free
the price
is high
but payable

so measure out
what it means
to be in the room
packed in
with the other smiles
and still
be
invisible

count the cost
of showing up
in order to remain
unseen
taped shut

decide for yourself
if you can afford

this inflation of acceptance
an eternal tariff on attachment

tally the total:
you know, don't you
the price
has always been
your soul?

so decide where the devil dwells
exactly—
in the deals rubber-stamped under
steeples
where you turn in your freedom
to become a righteous slave
or
in the wild woods under moonlight
where the going rate is
wrestle
wrestle
wrestle
your way
to a new name
in an old skin

for the ones who have been certain
and now are not

if I could breathe
the blowzy
dandelion froth
up high
and have you learn
all the strange
and crazy reasons
why

I'd wish instead
you'd know
a love so deeply safe
you'd go

on living
w i d e
without
those crystal
answers

I'd show you—
it's the
questions
that turn us into
dancers

permission slip

if waves of anxiety
come crashing
from an endless ocean

if dissatisfaction
is a half-hearted
sensation

if the harsh dissonance
of idealism
rings through
your real, right-now life

if deciding what you want
or knowing what you need
is just too massive a demand

know this:

you are allowed to
simply
be
where you are
with what you have

resources may be
u n l i m i t e d
your ability to receive them
isn't

so ignore
the hawking
of the try-harder sales pitches

tune out
the voices
of the ever-urgent time-saviors

dial down
the deception that says
reveling in this ripening moment
is insufficient

you are acceptable
even as
your misbehaving self
with your un-brave face
and your worst-laid plans

you have permission to
simply
be
where you are
with what you have

scars

invisible brands
are the worst kind
because they still burn
like scorched skin
but no one knows
you felt the heat
and no one
sees the scars

savage heart

when the limits
loom
large and long
across your fields

each bitter barb
caging
the wild animal of your
savage and beautiful
heart

watch your fenced-in
sense of freedom
pace
and fret
and grow languid
with the longing
scratching at patches
of earth, snuffing
at the breath of breezes
haunting
the hem of the sphere

do not miss it:
you are teaching
your soul to
f l y

these obscene edges
have gifted you
a stubborn spine
and ceaseless spirit
unyielding ferality
to search
        seek
              find
a firm foundation
from which to
              l e a p
and live beyond
eternal wire

a blessing for the bully in your head

I can't help but think
this wasn't what you had in mind for us...
is it?

By now, you believed, by now
surely
all the pieces would be in place.

By now, we'd see
something whole,
instead of holes punching through,
like our goal was confetti.

This is why…
all that blame
all that shame
all that belittlement
of the battles that we fight

and why you've burned a brand
blue hot
into the blessed skull surrounding us.

Oh, beloved.

May you breathe deep
the fragrance of the fresh-cut
green
that struggles up through soil
only to be cut down again
scorched and withered
again
crushed and conquered
again.

May you pull close
a promise:
resurrections only come for
those who die.

May you sense space
to surrender the agenda
resounding with your
fear
and feel permission
to be at peace,
abounding with fierce
self-grace.

May you believe,
my outcast's advocate,
all earning is unnecessary
to gain a given love.

for the love

i.

we would have given
everything

—we did give everything—

so we could be loved

ii.

because they told us
what they'd been told:
nothing
is enough
for a theism
thirsting
to drink you dry

because they told us
we can't come as we are
unless we are ready
to change when we get there

because they told us
unless we are less
we cannot have more

unless we take out our hearts
and burn them on an altar
we cannot belong

unless we scrape
every last scrap of desire
from between our teeth
bleed every last artery
dry of ambition
corral every last thought
from possibility of imagination

we cannot be loved

iii.

tell me, when will we start saying
'controlled' instead of 'loved'
since that is what we mean?

iv.

they said it
            as if we deserved all this shame
                        this shame
                 this shame

as if our own precious names
would always be lies

v.

they told us
we couldn't earn it
but here is what we must do to keep it
and they said we've been given it
but the strings attached
will strangle with
one
wrong
move

the words ring from the wooden stages
and the promises dangle at our nostrils

come
just come
and do
and change
and get. in. line.
and then
you will be loved

we were the puppets
and their acceptance
twitched our strings

vi.

but now dear one
now
the strings are snipped
by your scissors of self-kindness

there are no more stages
you were never meant to be
a puppet, but a
bird broken free
and you have always been loved

vii.

your own love
holds you
so unfailingly
and will now
never change

and when you seize this cup
swallow down every drop
y o u
will change

you will become
the unabridged version
of who you are

you will learn
you are allowed
to love yourself

and when you do
you'll find
that's all you really ever wanted

alive

do you feel
that cracking apart

hull
splitting

a coming alive
by way of death

we are changing

these borders
are broadening
rivering
like spilled milk
uncontained
untamed

no getting it back

love,
cry all you want

ache is a passport

I.

let the ache
e c h o
through and through
every slice in your skin
every scar on your soul
every sinkhole in your heart

let the ache
reverberate
across the ceiling of your mind, thrum
through the sinuous asylum
of your lungs, ring
round the rioting
in the streets of your thighs, sink
muffled
into the cold places
of your feet

and
     ache
         ache
            ache

II.

know the sting
feel it
slide your fingers
along it's every
jagged edge
listen
to what this dying past
is breathing with her last

memorize this pain

never forget
how it feels
to be
silent

III.

the ache
is the answer

because this pain
is a passport

out of what's wrong
and into your rights

IV.

hush

try
try to breathe

pull it in
—precious air
inflating the space
built to burst your voice
alive
and free

feel it in your bones
spasms of expansion
overrunning
stoic border
control

an emigrating
desire
is restamping the codes and
red-inking
a way out

so, ache
ache
ache

until the throbbing
shatters
the cage
keeping
all of you
in

free fall

now that your faith
is floating
away
on a fresh breeze
             you'll grow wingtips
           where you used to heft
                 weights
                       and the free fall
                            will begin
                               to feel
                            like flight

red pin

i almost told you
to go find
someone
who can become
your red pin
on the map of life
a marker meaning home
curved 3D beacon
calling you
across
a flat earth

but then i remembered
all the good words
about being at home
with yourself
because you're the only one
who will spend
every
sacred
second
with you
and i changed my mind

no forfeit

beloved
your
past pain
present opinions
future failures

do not define

who you are
who you're meant to be
who you will become

you are held
held
h e l d

in the arms of a
welcoming
world

you don't
forfeit
your value
because
someone else did

you don't
lose
your identity
because
no one else recognizes
who you are

you don't
give up
your peace
because
others panic
about their own doubt

you are held
held
h e l d
by this moment in time

and you don't have to be
someone else
to be loved

trespassers will be composted

the falsehoods they planted
lodged down
deep
into the foundation
because we were terrified
they were true

but those lies won't thrive
here
in this liberated land

so rip out their fear-fed roots
name your soil
as your own
put up a heretic scarecrow
and a 'no trespassing' sign

what you've found
cost far too much
to let false witnesses
sow invasive
seeds
of shame

satisfaction

if i could tell you
they will apologize someday
'come around' someday
shift and change and own their shit
someday—

if i could tell you
everyone will see
how they screwed you up and over
lied through wide, loud mouths
and left you limping—

if i could tell you
the audience will quit calling
the stagemen heroes
when they aren't
and finally, someone will dig out the dirt
under the carpet—

i would

but i can't

you and me, we may live
the rest of our days
without that settlement

but let's be damned
before we let
their scrunch-eyed scarcity
subvert
our satisfying
now

what was stolen

all
stolen from you
is irreplaceable

please

honor this
appropriately—
with spurts of anger
and reams of rage
and swollen bottles
inking tears

ii.

i know the words
about the crumbs
on the waves
but i am here to say
your bread does not
come back
because what was taken
is not what washes up—
only what you

cast and release
yourself

iii.

so weep
for what could have been
and is not

grieve
for everything stolen
that has been lost

mourn
every moment
never known
every moment
known too well

let grief
dig
a grave in you

iv.

keep
your
vigil

tolerate
no 'wise' counsel
telling you to

'move on'
move on

when you're ready
and not before

v.

if you want to,
plant
something
atop the place of interment

flowers
a flag
a fucking food truck

sprinkle your own, good
grace upon it
and grow your own, new
joy
from the ground up

dear daughter

you are allowed
to slice the apple
into pieces
cut the tight
blood-red skin
separate the whole
into halves
once bitten there is
no putting it back together

but do
plant the seeds
nest them gently
in sun-baked soil
rain down
the liquid of your love
shine the light
of your acceptance
upon the planted core
of you

and wait
and watch

tenderly tend
what is growing

shelter her through
the shift of these seasons
wrench out
all weeds of guilt
sown by anyone else
yank out
jealous thorns threatening
to choke out
this child-plant

nurture
your nature

nestle
into your knowing

take what was their fruit
and grow
down
your own wild roots

let them go

let them go
as they are

let them go
angry
lashing out
tantrumming
over what they wanted
and which you,
no longer a citizen of
their co-dependent state,
cannot
give them

let them go
confused
utterly dazed by
all
they will not know
baffled
by a language they
cannot wrap their tongues
around

let them go
disappointed

in the audacity
of your own sovereign
autonomy
dissatisfied by how
'you've changed'
as if allegiance to
their tyrannous opinions
was your personal
national debt

let them go
afraid
terrified
of the demons created
in their own image
and frightened
for the state of your soul
which they thought
they'd conquered
pierced with a flag
colonizing all curiosity
and killing off your rightful heir

let them go
passive-aggressive
stalking on socials
firing off unsolicited
phone calls of self-defense
and rounds of wrathful, ranting letters

44

to fortess
their own sense of
discomfort

let them go
cheerful
secretly smiling
at your supposed poverty
naively sure
of your return
to their bombed-out
blistered kingdom

let them go
silent
—
the ones who'd rather
grieve your death
than face the possibility
of your defection
or chance-encounter
their own error

let them go
empty-handed
offer no more
fistfuls
of your sacred soil

to carry in jars
and display as souvenirs

let them go
apathetic
uninterested
in your very existence
your own beautiful life
your own freeborn truth

let them go
let them go
let them
g o

this may be the hardest thing
you ever do
it may also be easier
than you expect

for who has time
to hate
when you're living
in delight?

maybe someday, when you're ready,
you'll let them go
as they are
in love

on the question, 'will it get easier?'

the past you've outgrown
will not stop fitting
too tightly

lost friendships
dead and buried
will not resurrect

you will still feel
phantom pains
of an amputated
identity

no, love.
it will not 'get easier'

but you, dearest…
you will grow stronger

you'll begin to
fill out
the loose seams
of your future

your own burned tongue
will taste the difference

between flavor
of friendship
and vinegar of
expectations

your skin will thicken
shielding
your soft and precious heart
from barbed words
arrowed at you

while the opinions of others
lose their weight
you'll grow lighter

the flatline of grief
will no longer have power
to fell you

your strength will become
easier to own
even if life itself
does not demand less

it will not get easier

but you, darling,
will grow stronger
and your strength

will invite freedom
and your freedom
will rhyme with 'happy'

breaking apart
does not get easier
but you
will finally catch the light
coming through
the cracks

acknowledgements // with deepest thanks to

Beverly Varnado. Your words in August 2021 turned *The Key to Everything* and unlocked a closet where the poems sat on a dusty shelf. I am forever grateful.

Sarah Spradlin. This thing wouldn't exist without you. Seriously. Thank you for being my personal cheer squad and editorial team!

The Group That Shall Not Be Named. You promised me I wasn't crazy. I believe you.

Deborah Blythe, Shar Busch, and Shari Kaplan. Your kindness in reading early drafts meant so much to me, and gave me the courage to continue.

David Tensen. Thank you for always believing I could do this, and for generously offering the tools to make it happen.

Kristin Vanderlip. I'm beyond grateful for your companionship along the writer's journey. Thank you that nothing was ever too small to celebrate, process, or vent about over Voxer.

My friends in The Poetry Pub, The Poetry Chapel Collective, and the old version of hope*writers. The communities we created together have given my writing life light + air. I'm thankful for you.

My retreat badasses: Danielle, Deepika, Marcy, Mav, Megs, Paula, Victoria. Thank you for letting me read so many of these pieces to you, and for telling me that my story matters.

My sons. You have the most beautiful, starry souls that were ever pinned down to the ground. Your interruptions were gifts, even when I didn't know it. Never believe anyone who says you are anything but good inside.

David. You are the best thing that's ever happened to me. All the poetry is insufficient. I love you infinity x infinity x gargantuan, to the gargantuan power, a lot of times—and after that, too.

about the author

Amanda Dzimianski [zhuh-man-skee] is a lifelong writer building a home in poetry, and a human learning how to be—how to be present, to be whole, to be loving, to be herself.
She is a certified writing coach, parent and partner, homeschool teacher, and a firm believer in the power of the small space.
She lives near Athens, Georgia, the lands of the Yuchi, Muskogee/Creek, and Cherokee (Eastern Band) peoples, with her spouse David and their two young sons.
You can connect with Amanda online at amandadzimianski.com, and on Instagram at @amanda.idareyoutospellit.

If you found the contents of this book meaningful...

would you consider leaving a review?

(I know, I know—it's more inconvenient than it should be, to be honest. But if you found some sort of solace in these pages, or a sense of being seen or heard, your review is one of the best ways to help others find and receive the same things.)

I'm grateful you spent your time reading these poems. Thank you.

Interested in coaching for your own writing or poetry?

Send Amanda an email:
amanda@amandadzimianski.com

or visit her coaching page:
amandadzimianski.com/coaching.

She loves to help writers, poets, and entrepreneurs move out of overwhelm and into creative clarity.

Join The WIP (work-in-progress) List email family.

Subscribers receive fresh poetry, and are the first to hear about new projects.

Visit amandadzimianski.com/wip
to join for free.